Asa Livingston brings life to the colour spectrum as we know it; recounting glorious fables, dreadful tragedies, and tranquility within life's simple moments — connected by colours of every hue imaginable. For as many colours exist, there are as many, or more, beautiful stories for your mind and heart to feast on in this Gathering of Miniature Tales.

Arian Derwydd Books, LLC

https://arianderwyddbooks.com/

Part One—The Regulars

Pink

Pink is her skin.

Pink is her strong tail.

Pink are the scales upon her chest and hips.

Pink are her eyes; bold and lustful.

Pink braids wrapped in seaweed sprout from her scalp.

Pink are her sharp fingernails, too.

Pink is even her last name!

Pink is also her aura; loving and passionate.

Pink are the pearls she loves.

Pink is her heart, yearning for true love.

Pink are the seas that float within her soul.

Pink ribbons drape the walls of the lobby.

Pink champagne bottles sit idly by on ice.

Pink sheets lay over the gift tables.

Pink napkins, folded like butterflies hold silverware on white plates.

Pink t-shirts and accessories lay on a pink table by the window.

Pink handkerchiefs are worn by friends.

Pink wigs are worn by some young daughters.

Pink are the ribbon pins stapled to everyone.

Pink awareness for the fallen graces the causal room.

Pink are the hearts of the supporting caregivers.

Pink is breast cancer awareness.

Pink eyes.

Pink lips.

Pink tulle on her dress.

Pink ribbons in her dark hair.

Pink roses in her slim hands.

Pink, puffy clouds soar above her.

Pink is her aura; loving and sweet.

Pink candies in her plump purse.

Pink kitten heeled shoes with bows sat on her feet.

Pink cheeks flush at the sight of her beloved family.

Pink joy surrounds her; she has found love at last.

Red

Red was his car.

Red lips marked his cheeks.

Red leather made his clothes.

Red leaves fell from dozy trees.

Red sand covered his shoes.

Red sunsets were adored by him.

Red carpets dressed his home's floors.

Red velvet cupcakes were a must in his kitchen.

Red consumed his being; it was his favourite color.

Red cherries and apples were also admired.

Red tongues slurped up strawberry ice cream.

Red hair clogged his shower drain.

Red walls built his home and mind.

Red was him.

Red is the blood on his hands.

Red stains linger on his weapon.

Red fires still swallow the remains of the village.

Red rivers of cold fluids seep into the grounds.

Red, raging flames burn inside him; this betrayal of the most intimate.

Red vengeance most foul shall rain upon them all.

Red birds chirp their cheerful tunes.

Red trees grow to enormous sizes.

Red sand deserts sit close to the gigantic forest.

Red sports cars race on mountain side roads.

Red ferns grow along dirt paths.

Red sunsets shine over the neighboring seas.

Red swarms of fish scatter within.

Red stars light the night sky.

Orange

Orange is the colour of her jazzy dress.

Orange feathers stand from her brown braids.

Orange beads make her sparkle.

Orange banners and drapes of tulle create the stage's backdrop.

Orange streamers, napkins, and placemats decorate the audience's tables.

Orange signs screaming her name greet viewers at the doorway.

Orange suits and silver dresses are worn by employees of the club in her honor.

"Orange you glad to be here, too?" a host asks.

"Orange skies of fire light up my heart…" Miss Angeline sings.

Orange song notes dwell in her heart and soul, forevermore.

Orange was the fruit.

Orange was her shirt.

Orange wasn't her favourite colour, though; it was his.

Orange trees covered his garden in shade.

Oranges fill Trevon's fruit bowl every year.

Orange was the colour of his pants, looking like amber.

Orange were his bright kitchen cabinets; Annette loved them.

Orange was his car; such a weird colour for such a classy thing.

Orange, the many shades of it filled his space.

Orange—according to him—was simple, yet boisterous and delicious!

Orange trees thrive on the evergreen hills.

Orange juice is produced by them.

Orange summer dresses are worn by the drinkers.

Orange packets of sweet chocolates are devoured by the children with them.

Orange glass dishware holds the peoples' meals; the kids get plastic versions.

Orange clouds bid the overhead sun 'good night.'

Orange-clad party goers build a bonfire to continue their stay.

Orange sunrises greet the beloved trees the very next day.

Yellow

Yellow was her soul, vibrant and bouncy like her wavy red curls.

Yellow paint covered her house.

Yellow was her favourite colour, next to sky blue.

Yellow, the sun was that day she fell in love with herself.

Yellow was the colour of her favourite sundress that had pockets!

Yellow were the flowers around her home.

Yellow bed sheets and soft blankets were in her bedroom.

Yellow lemonade and lemon pastries sat on her kitchen counters.

Yellow sunglasses sat on her nose when she traveled.

Yellow was her aura anywhere she went, as cheerful as the Spring.

Yellow is the sun shining in the blue sky above.

Yellow are the parrots flying by amongst the trees.

Yellow is her flowing gown; silky and billowing behind her feet.

Yellow is her now dusty skin.

Yellow tinted are her hazel eyes.

Yellow flowers crown her fluffy, brunette hair.

Yellow fluids leave her sickly… but not ill enough to not enjoy her last vacation.

Yellow was the moon that night the yellow sickness held her powerless.

Yellow was a favourite colour of hers… even when it consumed her.

Yellow and black bees buzz from wildflower to wildflower.

Yellow flies and wasps join their feasting.

Yellow daffodils and sunflowers wait their turn to give the pollinators assistance.

Yellow nectar from them all is unwasted; the bugs thrive on it.

Yellow honeycombs await; the sweet honey is the fruit of the bees' labour.

Yellow sun rays shine on them all for guidance.

Green

Green is envy and grass.

Green is her glorious gown.

Green carpets lead the way to her throne.

Green jewels and snakes decorate the mighty chair.

Green is powerful... for those who have the diamond.

Green is said to be divine, according to the peasant folk.

Green was once claimed long ago by a powerful king, declaring himself a demigod.

Green graced his halls of steel and stone.

Green was, thereafter, taken by her as a wish to be as powerful as he was.

Green — the colour is nothing without the cosmic jewel.

Green-clad soldiers belonging to her inspect every corner of the world for it.

Green neon lights glow on the posters on the wall.

Green words flutter away from the old gramophone in the corner of the space.

Green lipstick is painted on her thick lips.

Green, dingy carpet soaks up another coffee stain by the kitchenette.

Green bracelets are on her wrists… they can't sit still.

Green fingers dance on white and black keys, making green notes to join the words already in the air.

Green melodies come from her apartment henceforth.

Green nights in the city are not uncommon.

Green fans love hearing her practice when it's late at night; it's soothing.

Green concerts are beloved by many.

Green wannabes try to copy her style, but just become inspired instead.

Green songs happily fly everywhere in the state now.

Green noxious gases drift in the dreary skies.

Green, rank fluids wash the desolate streets.

Green storm clouds bring acid rain to the radioactive lands.

Green mists hover over toxic ponds and lakes.

Green, tainted plants struggle to adapt to the desecrated environments.

Green, envious, careless humans wrought this tragedy upon them all; no one will miss them.

Green, sickly roses hope for a brighter future.

"One day." They dream. "One day."

Teal

Teal are his eyes, with snake-like pupils.

Teal gloves cover his slender hands.

Teal scales grace his high cheekbones.

Teal shoes sit over his reptilian feet.

Teal tiles decorate his small abode.

Teal memories of his old home in the sea float in his mind.

Teal waters of tropical lands birthed him and his family.

Teal is his heart—reminiscent of bygone days.

"Teal. His shirt was teal," she informs the officer.

Teal fabric makes Macey's shirt, too; funny that.

"Teal shirt, dark blue pants, white shoes?" Detective Stafford inquires.

Teal water barrels sit idly by; a few turquoise scales hide beside them, unseen.

Teal waters of the bay splash against the bridge.

Teal notes are scribbled on Stafford's notepad; she can't believe what she hears.

"Teal was his skin! I could've sworn it!" Miss Macey yips.

"Teal? For sure?" Stafford questions again with an eyebrow raised this time.

"Teal! Yes! He is a good friend of mine — and he's missing!" Macey confirms, nearly pleading.

Teal beetles scurry down the walls of the alley in silence.

Teal eyes scan for movement in the dim room.

Teal feet shuffle in the snug space; they need moisture.

Teal lungs seek more oxygen to breathe.

Teal arms grow weary from being shackled and scratched.

Teal, delicate skin wrinkles in the dry air of the empty warehouse.

Teal scales fall off of him, like crumbs from a cookie; they need to be followed.

Teal gills gasp for water.

Teal bugs and grey rats are the only company… besides the savages that stole him.

Teal prayers to his goddess are whispered in between beatings from the monsters.

Teal questions arise from Tan'ala's crisp lips: "What do they want from me? What did I do? Whyy???"

Teal cries call for help, but he's too deep inside the cage of this blasted prison.

Teal dreams of freedom drift into the night… maybe… maybe a friend will help.

Blue

Blue is the lively ocean.

Blue is their hair, flowing in the wind like waves.

Blue — the colour of their clothes — comfortable and light.

Blue skies poured from the heavens, dotted with puffy white clouds floating above.

Blue was a state of mind.

Blue is their life.

Blue is the water that makes them.

Blue is all life.

Blue, blue nights sat patiently around the home.

Blue silk pajamas were worn by him.

Blue snowflakes fell upon the soft snow.

Blue drinking glasses were still on his mahogany desk.

Blue decorations of tulle and sparkling tree ornaments were sprawled around the living space.

Blue dinner plates covered the dark dining table, now clean after the party.

Blue curtains draped beside the back window where he stood, watching.

Blue heartbeats tapped his ribs; if only they could be freed.

Blue teardrops stood at the ducts' edges; they needed to fall.

Blue was her gown and skin.

Blue lights lit up the club's dance room.

Blue eyes watched her sway to the groovy music.

Blue screens played music videos for observers.

Blue incense burners filled the air with the sweet scents of flowers.

Blue crystals glowed on shelves and tables for ambiance.

Blue music notes brought joy to the people here!

Purple

Purple was her hair and the flowers within.

Purple her gown, elegant in its form, graced the cobalt floors of her foyer.

Purple were the eyes of her beloved.

Purple burned in Anastasia's heart.

Purple was her favourite colour.

Purple filled the air around the wedding.

Purple — like lilacs and lavender — filled her lungs.

Purple surrounded the loving couple… until the day they died.

Purple… the colour of love.

Purple eyes scoured the busy landscape.

Purple errors kept appearing by the ever-changing information captured.

Purple ribbons entangled her shifting fingers.

Purple nerves scattered over her shining skin.

Purple strings held her grey braids in place on her head.

Purple hearts danced in her mind, pulsing with every shift.

Purple neon lights lit her train's path.

Purple night skies laid ahead.

Purple heroes waited there… She was waiting there.

Purple roses led her astray.

Purple hydrangeas fenced in the pathway.

Purple silk lilies were tied to dark trees.

Purple stepping stones made her waltz across the sparkling pond.

Purple rugs with runes welcomed her to the other side, enchanting Lonna in the forest's beauty.

Purple bricks became visible through the dirt of the path; they hid spells on their surfaces.

Purple mist rose around the violet cottage, hiding his lair from her.

Purple specters haunted the exterior of the seemingly little building.

Purple doors drew Lonna inside; the interior of the house was hidden in shadow.

Purple goblins joyfully greeted her; they couldn't wait for their queen.

Purple, bizarre eyes popped out of a dark room; a purple satin suit followed soon after.

"Purple roses, as you ordered, my sweet," he softly uttered, bowing. "I pray you stay. I've missed you," Verol whispered; his gaze lost inside of her.

Purple magic flowed from his love's fingertips, making flower petals fall at his feet; her delicate hand caressed his cheek as he smiled.

Purple roses are her favourite, he remembered; forever and always.

Brown

Brown is the mud beneath his feet.

Brown are his boots, and more so thanks to the sloppy dirt.

Brown, the colour of his eyes and hair.

Brown and scarlet are the leaves on the trees around him.

Brown is his last name; Andrew is his first.

Brown was the folder he dropped off at the library yesterday.

Brown was the suit he wore to the gala the night before.

Brown, the colour of his wife's gown, too.

Brown is her hair colour as well, but much darker.

Brown — like dust — is his.

Brown is the trail to their house.

Brown is humble, like he is; he's thankful for all he has.

Brown hair swirls in the heavy wind.

Brown dust trails guide her lover's red car to her.

Brown and grey cobblestones fence her warm house.

Brown vines in slumber cover them all.

Brown music notes fly from her beloved's lips as he
greets her after parking.

Brown rugs inside welcome his feet back into her
abode; it's been a while.

Brown colleges and studies kept him away, stealing his
mind and heart for a bit.

Brown cushions of her couch hold heart-shaped
pillows atop of them.

Brown eyes glance at the man's luggage, hoping he
remains this time.

Brown silks in her room frame the windows,
protecting their secrets.

Brown lipstick plants love's marks on his neck.

Brown warm hugs envelope his torso.

Brown joy has reunited the couple.

Brown certificates tell her that he's staying... finally forever.

Brown hooves stamp footprints into the grass below them.

Brown, dirty hair attracts fleas to feed.

Brown and white patterns dot the young mare's coat.

Brown eyes spot a plaything in the field before her.

Brown-clad caretakers watch Georgie as she races to the giant ball with excitement.

Brown gloves protect the carer's hands as she shovels horse waste into a barrel for composting.

Brown dung will be used to fertilize Tracy's fields this year.

Brown snorts of joy come from Georgie; she is thankful for the new toy!

Brown boots tread towards the pair.

Brown and black hair of another horse rider joins Tracy and Georgie.

Brown-black hooves of a Friesian lad join the scene; he will be a new friend for Georgie!

Black

Black — like twilight — was her skin; 'twas sleek as oil.

Black were her eyes.

Black was the coal in her hands, prepared to be lit.

Black is the soul inside her, still.

Black holes filled her heart after that fateful night.

Black ashes remained.

Black shadows taint her skin, though barely visible to the naked eye.

Black skies flood her memory, poisoning her sanity.

Black was the girl that set fire to the capital.

Black shadows dart across the wall.

Black hair of the investigator swings as they move their head over to see.

Black flashlights search for the culprit.

Black boots take tender steps to follow the sounds.

Black daggers find them instead.

Black pools appear in the dark edges of the complex.

Black rooms quickly become lighter, revealing the bloodied bodies.

Black leather of the 'gator's gloves reaches…

Black arms of a murderer.

Black clad bodies fight for power; he won't get away this time.

Black bruises and bloody noses join the scene.

Black guns end the brawl.

Black was his skin; he was her shadow.

Blackened were the corpses; it was too late for them.

Black linen hid his face; there's no stopping now.

"BlackHeart! Where are you?! I can smell you!", the silver woman screeched, pacing. "Get over here!"

Black words dripped from her tongue.

"BlackHeart... I will kill you one of these days."

BlackHeart, the assassin, slipped into another dark space behind some boxes.

Blackened stone walls contained the feud.

Black rubble was crushed by the shining villainess.

"BlackHeart?" the woman called again.

Black poison laced her lustrous sword.

Black sweat fell into his eyes; she was too close.

Black heartbeats raced through his chest.

Black muscles tightened as the decision was made.

BlackHeart sped to the crumbling doorway.

"Black!" She noticed him.

Black shoes carried him to his split-second freedom; he was almost there.

Black skies hung over the chase.

BlackHeart was as good as dead; Venna'lin was an excellent warrior.

Silver light caught his eyes; her sword caught his heart.

Black venom seared his aching muscle; silver smiles enjoyed it.

Grey

Grey was his robe.

Grey was his beard; he could've been easily mistaken
as a wizard.

Grey was the Order's colour; simplicity was key.

Grey with flecks of blue were his eyes.

Grey stones made the building.

Grey, grand archways greeted the elders every day.

Grey shadows of previous guild members and visitors
sweep the deep halls.

Grey tablets of clay were stored in a great
underground library, recording the history of the
village.

Grey stories of love and war were encased in the flat
books.

Grey figures make sure their people know where they
have come from, and to not repeat the disasters of their
ancestors.

Grey beads lay on the marble floor.

Grey stripes in the tiles point to the red puddle close by.

Grey fabric covered her cadaver; poor thing.

Grey hair once neatly tied up on her scalp sits beside her head in limp waves on the ground.

Grey wool coats sit in the scene on boxes.

Grey suits of investigators scour the area for more clues.

Grey shadows were seen earlier by customers of the shop.

Grey rain clouds hung over the brick building of Poinsettia Hall.

Grey faces of the witnesses mourn for the victim, Ms. Pearl.

Grey notebooks kept records of the statements.

Grey minds examine plausible scenarios of what happened earlier.

Grey vehicles gather the inspectors with the evidence to take them back to their offices.

Grey pigeons watch from a power line across the street — like an audience.

Grey space explorers target a new world to visit; they are bored from the monotonous trading with their allies.

Grey minds tire easily with schedules.

Grey star ports get bland rather quickly when one is as intelligent as they are.

Grey are their clothes, too; one requires no flashy fashion when traveling between solar systems.

Grey minds need colour in this vast, kaleidoscopic universe — not grey, drab boxes.

Grey souls do not exist, for souls only exist in full colour!

White

White was the blood-stained snow.

White were the clouds above.

White was the sword in his hand, matching his armor.

White were the woman's wings, glorious with soft feathers.

White was the light sent from her protector.

White, the colour of her blood.

White was all he saw that day.

White filled his mind.

White filled her heart and soul.

White was his face once she finally attacked.

Red poured from within him.

Red… she didn't like thenceforth.

White was her colour, as was his… but things change.

White ghosts float around her; they bring bad
memories of the past.

White sparks of her electric dagger fall on her skin.

White scars glow on her arms and hands, reminiscent
of the power she once had.

White cotton sheets protect her weapons from the
musty air of her cabin.

White flowers wilt in a glass vase on her windowsill.

White cobwebs not yet torn down hide in hidden areas
of Adella's things.

White canvas fabrics dress her furniture.

White metal armor lay in pieces on a table to be
cleaned.

White sunlight of a new day shines in her space,
illuminating the dust and gnats within.

White little spiders watch their meals fly into their
nests.

White clouds float in the skies above, puffier than ever.

White fields of snow-topped meadows glisten in the
sun's rays, now at peace.

White-tailed deer scavenge in the nearby woods,

hoping for something to eat this morning.

White currents of electricity run through her veins—

finally not for fighting—but adjusting to this new

feeling.

White steel shines in the morning sunlight.

White stones inlaid glimmer in the rays; the new details show her life story.

White-tipped hair is braided and placed in loops atop her head.

White, silk gloves cover her scarred hands.

White battle paint covers Adella's lips and cheeks.

White are her unwavering eyes.

White linen strips are wrapped around the powerful weapon she holds.

White sparks try to escape her blade but are contained within the confines of the fabric.

White orbs of vast proportions bloom in the blue skies above her; they have come.

"White Gods of Light, receive my call!" she bellows to the anomaly. "My duty is done." She bows, offering her sword. Adella looks up at the gods, and exhales, "You can have it back; I don't need it anymore."

White spirits appear before her; they hear her enervation.

White nebulous hands reach for the blade; the fingers are slim.

White energy consumes the small space around the sword; they have it.

White is Adella's face; she's never been this close to the gods before!

White power bursts as they leave her; her body — startled — jumps back.

White clouds cover the group as they bid her farewell.

"White Warrior... you shall be forevermore venerated throughout history," they called to her, they didn't mean to spook her.

"White Warrior Adella, you will be missed once you're through," they added. "We'll make sure you're well cherished until then," one being kindly said with a faint wink.

Part Two—The Metallics

Gold

"Gold was his heart!" she wept, wiping water off her soft face.

Gold statues, figurines, and trinkets sat by her feet.

Gold jewelry and golden shoes decorated her body.

"Gold? How are you so sure?" the mortician asked with empty eyes.

Gold clad crowds stood near the funeral space, with offerings at the ready in their hands.

Gold light from the sun shone upon the mourning kingdom.

"Gold!" she bellowed through streams of tears.

"Gold was his heart! There's nothing you could ever do to take my heart away from that thought!" she finally cried before breaking.

Gold was her husband, the king.

Golden sun rays pierced the veil of the stormy weather.

Gold armor glistened in the warm light as he stepped forward.

Gold was the cool space he stood in, reflecting his soul.

"Gold was his heart," they said; "Gold wasn't his heart" is what the others said…

Gold hearts matter not to the gods of old.

Gold souls are worth more.

Golden swords cut nothing with power.

Gold-plated steel protects no one from the wrath.

Golden fingers touch only those deserving of the mighty.

Golden shoes merely walk into darkness, not light.

Gold-brimmed glasses seek only lust.

Gold flakes do not help lips taste life, but sadly kiss death.

Golden trumpets are not to be used for the victory of men; they are the knells for the Damned.

Golden flowers carry no sweet smell for the greedy.

Golden minds do not exist, for there is no physical enlightenment.

Golden existence is exclusively granted from the gods themselves… for those who are worthy of such sanctity.

Silver

Silver strings of fabric clung to the broken architecture.

Silver beams worn down by the foul weather creaked as she stood powerful.

Silver hair of her scalp flowed in the wind, like a banner.

Silver armor gleamed in the scattered sunlight.

Silver swords and arrows sat on her hips and back.

Silver gashes were carved into her iron shell.

Silver blood spilled from minor cuts on her skin.

Silver chalices of fresh wine were taken to her as peace offerings.

Silver soldiers under the metal maiden's rule destroyed them, knowing that the wine inside was poisoned.

Silver eyes watched the peasants try to make a truce with her; a simple compromise gone awry.

Silver creatures do not need to force the hand of men anymore but try to coexist.

Silver disagreements with long blades said otherwise.

Silver blood shall rule in the end… not red.

Silver in sheen were the clotted clouds.

Silver was his toga and wings.

Silver were his wrist braces; he needed braces for his feathers instead.

Silver was his name written down in history; a significant role to humans… not so much to the gods.

Silver melted into his bones, 'twas too hot.

Silver was the golden sun's discouraged heart.

Silver were the screams.

Silver was his downfall… What a shame…

Icarus.

Silver was the material needed.

Silver were the chains.

Silver was her heart's cage.

Silver in colour was his armor and polearm; he was the guard to watch her.

Silver bars held Beulah prisoner; they claimed it was for her safety.

Silver spires towered over the barricaded city.

Silver streets were dug into the soil so no plant could live within; 'twas a dreary sight.

Silver jails were to be expanded with the help of her hand.

Silver and other metals were easily manipulated by Beulah.

Silver-clad rulers of the scene wished she would help, but it was to no avail.

Silver-bending Beulah was not to be trifled with.

Copper

Copper coins cover the bayside dock.

Copper pans are used by the chef cooking up a fresh catch.

Copper forks dig into the finished appetizers; the salads of flavours are delicious!

Copper statues stare at the foodies below their gazes.

Copper eyes of the magician watch the colourful ingredients burst into art.

Copper buttons close his dapper, teal waistcoat.

Copper spoons stir his milky tea.

Copper pans hold his cooking, fluffy eggs.

Copper chisels help carve miniature statues out of clay.

Copper monocles are collected by him; they are only to be worn on special occasions.

Copper canes and bifocals sit in his ornate office; it is very refined with the best literature there is!

Copper tiles cover the study's ceiling.

Copper candlesticks hold melting vanilla-scented candles that make the room smell scrumptious.

Copper is versatile but remains a fleeting metal to be cherished as long as it lasts.

Copper wires make its hair.

Copper tubes lay on its back.

Copper sheets make up its body.

Copper fingers grasp at anything near.

Copper hinges hold everything in place.

Copper circuits drive electricity to every moving part
of its being.

Copper feet tread as lightly as it can towards new
friends.

Copper hearts are lined with gold as the wandering
robot experiences life like a living entity.

Bronze

Bronze statues in the courtyard.

Bronze busts in the foyer.

Bronze weapons in the armory.

Bronze breastplates cover the mens' chests.

Bronze-coloured plants sit in brass pots at the entrance.

Bronze jewelry decorate Tertius' wife; her flowing
gowns require the best of Rome's baubles!

Bronze just came into style not too long ago, so now
everyone who can afford it, loves it!

Bronze toner is smeared onto her skin.

Bronze highlights are added to her beachy hair.

Bronze eyes stare through hers as they focus on the chosen makeup.

Bronze models await her arrival; she is the star of the magazine.

Bronze and golden medals sit on Serenity's shelves in her house.

Bronze swimsuits are worn by the fashionistas as they pose for the cameras.

Bronze sunlight glimmers over the seaside town.

Bronze warmth of the bright day fades as the night sneaks in; it was a good day for the fancy ladies.

Bronze medallions hide in the weathered chest.

Bronze cannons succumb to desperate coral; metal things give them a safe space to live.

Bronze armor gives way to the rolling tides.

Bronze dishware stays put in their old cupboards.

Bronze spearheads watch the wooden poles wither away; plant matter can't stay too long in the open ocean.

Bronze-seeking divers visit the decrepit site for amusement.

Bronze coins and buttons are taken ashore from the shipwreck.

Bronze antiques are valuable to those who appreciate them.

Bronze Age artifacts are admired by both land beings and sea creatures!

Part Three—The Compounds

Sage

Sage green stones grant wishes to newcomers.

Sage minds protect the shrine the glossy genies reside in.

Sage followers of the mindful clan of Seekers help those in need.

Sage plants grow in tidy gardens with statues.

Sage green wood timbers make the peaceful structure.

Sage moss grows on riverside rocks downstream.

Sage kimonos are worn by lady visitors when spring comes around.

Sage baskets filled with flowers are gifted to the hospice.

Sage hearts are filled with care and kindness every year.

Sage leaves were dried in the morning light.

Sage herbs were planted in her garden.

Sage green buckets held mindless weeds.

Sage-seasoned pork meat was cooked in the kitchen for lunch.

Sage cookbooks held her mother's recipes.

Sage-filled canisters were sold to customers at the market.

Sage-flavoured candies were made every week for free samples.

Sage-coloured potware was used to make the best meals and products.

Sage-minded Martha always tried her best for her community!

Sage green lily pads floated in the still pond.

Sage willow trees fenced the area.

Sage moss covered wet rocks on the water's edge.

Sage frogs croaked love songs every night.

Sage cattails hid bugs' lairs from hunting birds.

Sage green grass grew lush from the nutritious soil.

Sage owls watched over the space as the moon rose over the tranquil scene.

Chartreuse

Chartreuse skin.

Chartreuse curves.

Chartreuse lips.

Chartreuse love — though bitter in its taste — lingers.

Chartreuse smoke fills the air around her.

Chartreuse eyelids hide potent green eyes with thin pupils.

Chartreuse poison drips from her fingertips, burning his supple skin.

Chartreuse acid flows through Da'lexi's tender shell.

Chartreuse — her toxic colour — penetrates his heart and flesh.

Chartreuse spines cover the plant's mouth.

Chartreuse toxins spill from its leaves, causing unaware insects to crawl inside.

Chartreuse roots dig into the soft soil beneath this monstrous flower.

Chartreuse grass sits around it, just breathing in the cozy air.

Chartreuse leaves cover grand silver-barked trees.

Chartreuse-tipped feathers fly about as a parrot swings by the scene.

Chartreuse poison dart frogs ribbit their bold songs to them all.

Chartreuse sunsets arrive in the forest scenery; another day is gone.

Chartreuse beasts rummage through the grimy garbage dumpsters.

Chartreuse weeds stare in wonder nearby; shame that such nutritious food scraps are set to rot away.

Chartreuse neon signs flicker their sad tunes of negligence.

Chartreuse poisoned water flood rain drains; luckily, the toxins will not flow anywhere else after tonight.

Chartreuse stars glimmer in hope for the unbalanced city.

Chartreuse gangs tear up the streets every week without shame.

Chartreuse cop cars do their best to capture the rascals.

Chartreuse trees dot the busy town providing shade for walking travelers.

Chartreuse billboards promote peace and desired products.

Chartreuse window screens hide sleeping denizens.

Chartreuse bugs watch it all collide in this weird metropolis of the rich, poor, and desperate people.

Marigold

Marigold flower fields fill the scene.

Marigold-coloured wine glasses are used as props for the dramatic moment.

Marigold-yellow roses are wrapped into a crown for her head.

Marigolds themselves make his crown.

Marigold-loving characters drink their summer wine as the audience croons.

Marigold curtains stand by for the scenes ending.

Marigold dramas speak of love and loss throughout the little town.

Marigold sunflowers dance in the breeze.

Marigold wheat grows ripe in the sunlight.

Marigold flower fields grow in patches in the farmer's land; several grow close to his house.

Marigold straw hats are worn by him and his sons.

Marigold crowns are made by his daughters; everyone in his family has one!

Marigold sunrises shine in the cool mornings.

Marigold sun rays grant life to the man's ecosystem.

Marigold bushes grow by his dear wife's grave; they were her favourite flower.

Marigold yellow permeates everything in their life.

Marigold-coloured cheese of the dish is all nice and browned.

Marigold yellow butter is glazed over the fellow buns.

Marigold, steamy corn cobs lay in a tray.

Marigold flowers stand proud in a vase in the middle of the table.

Marigold yellow placemats support white, square plates.

Marigold patterns burst from the floral tablecloth.

Marigold wheat bundles act as supporting centerpieces.

Marigold dinner options are not yet eaten by the family.

Marigold prayers are spoken; they are thankful for the feast.

Scarlet

Scarlet love.

Scarlet gown.

Scarlet Bloody Marys on the table.

Scarlet pasta sits before her seat, unfinished.

Scarlet kiss marks are left on her arm from her girlfriend.

Scarlet smiles last for days.

Scarlet wedding bells ring out in the distance.

Scarlet roses line their street in celebration of their jolly event.

Scarlet cakes are coveted by hungry guests.

Scarlet sheets of the couple's bed.

Scarlet hearts fly about their space.

Scarlet love stays forever for them.

Scarlet racing stripes cover the hood.

Scarlet leather suits sit in his wardrobe.

Scarlet rims are in the tires of his car.

Scarlet tattoos of wild flames sink into his skin.

Scarlet tigers are painted on the sides of the vehicle.

Scarlet heartbeats rage in his passionate chest.

Scarlet trophies gather dust on his shelves.

Scarlet tips in his hair speak of his glory days.

Scarlet footsteps shadow his stride as he reminisces about his racing tournaments.

Scarlet dreams of infinite sleek roads devour his thoughts every night.

Scarlet were his joyful early years.

Scarlet lilies grow from roadside ditches.

Scarlet butterflies and hummingbirds love to see them every morning now that they're blooming.

Scarlet insects feed from the fleeting flowers; a snack's a snack.

Scarlet ants have built a mountain near the weedy growths; more food for them!

Scarlet birds sit in the trees to watch the colourful parade.

Scarlet sunsets beckon the moon for another night.

Cerise

Cerise was her name, but not her colour.

Cerise was the seaweed surrounding her.

Cerise was the colour of her ex-husband's tail.

Cerise was the favourite colour of her child's.

Cerise schools of fish passed by her lilac tail.

Cerise shells were clipped into her silvery blonde hair.

Cerise paint covered the old diner's walls, chipped away by the rolling tides.

Cerise umbrellas reflected the hot sun's burning rays.

Cerise liked to visit the shorelines during her travels.

Cerise met her forever husband, Robbie, that way.

Cerise met him at a dock one night, and thought he was neat; they always met there thenceforth!

Cerise doorways.

Cerise brick walls.

Cerise linens.

Cerise roads leading to the Grand Hall.

Cerise bipedal beings cross fields to get to it.

Cerise hounds and livestock accompany the people.

Cerise banners and flags adorn their holy place.

Cerise flowers are planted in rows near the church.

Cerise disciples gather for assemblies in this beloved edifice.

Cerise lips touch a vacant heart.

Cerise fluids escape their fleshy prison.

Cerise hands tear at the meal's muscles.

Cerise bloodstains cover his satin shirt.

Cerise wine bottles lay in pieces all around the room.

Cerise drinks soak into the floor.

Cerise lies float carelessly in the air.

Cerise teeth dig into the luscious delicacy.

Cerise-blooded humans are too much to bear when
starving.

Cerise devils drown in ecstasy when feeding.

Cerise avengers won't catch him this time; they'll
blame someone else… like they do.

Cerise "vampires?" Nay, just a sneaky demon finding
someone to eat.

Burgundy

Burgundy lips and eyeshadow.

Burgundy-black hair frames her face.

Burgundy walls painted with blood hold the spider's web.

Burgundy silks drape her dusty breasts; the fabric is carefully fitted to her figure.

Burgundy spears and bows dangle in her lair.

Burgundy corpses lay alongside her pointed feet.

Burgundy-clad servants bid the queen a bountiful harvest; she and her cohorts will be hunting soon.

"Burgundy beverages are awaiting your tongue, milady," an abettor informs her.

Burgundy wines of blood and rotting grapes are admired by Queen Viviann.

Burgundy bloodshed is nigh for the enormous spiders...

Burgundy roses sit on her lap; they are for him.

Burgundy-leaved trees surround her.

Burgundy thoughts pester her mind; she is smitten.

Burgundy silk makes her slim dress.

Burgundy silk makes his nice shirt.

Burgundy velvet covers his car's seats.

Burgundy irises lay beside him as he drives.

Burgundy birds fly above them both; they belonged to the pair.

Burgundy hearts float around the couple as they meet.

Burgundy romance awaits…

Burgundy crayons were Darcy's favourite!

Burgundy skirts with big pleats stuffed her closet.

Burgundy sweaters and shirts filled drawers of dressers.

Burgundy dragon figurines were stacked on shelves.

Burgundy glassware was collected over the years.

Burgundy cat collars went from feline to feline; she had so many.

Burgundy barbecue sauce glazed chicken dinners.

Burgundy wines, sadly, were rejected by her tongue.

Burgundy tiles were painted on as a hobby.

Burgundy crafts eventually made their way to paying for her creative life.

Burgundy excitement for life fueled her through and through!

Magenta

Magenta eyes scan the horizon.

Magenta flowers bloom in the evening sunlight.

Magenta towers stand near him.

Magenta silks and linens with golden details cover him.

Magenta vines form his crown; he is the ruler of the Iris Faeries.

Magenta creatures bow to his presence.

Magenta petals sweep in via the southern breeze; his partner is coming.

Magenta love and loyalty rules over these lands… by the wedlock kings of Ruthen.

Magenta hair.

Magenta fingernails.

Magenta crocs with light pink and black socks.

Magenta tank tops paired with dark-wash blue jeans.

Magenta studded belts and clunky, black boots.

Magenta eyeshadows and lipsticks cover her face with black accents.

Magenta, floral patches were sewn onto her denim jacket.

Magenta flower crowns with dark gauges.

Magenta and black are a great, punky pair!

Magenta satin with pink tulle makes her gown.

Magenta roses and carnations sit in several vases in the crowded room.

Magenta drapes hide open windows.

Magenta, flat tennis shoes protect her feet; cute heels would hurt them.

Magenta violins play cheerful tunes for guests.

Magenta drinks are served to everyone.

Magenta cupcakes are offered to those with sweet teeth.

Magenta games busy bored visitors.

Magenta dresses are worn by some close friends.

Magenta streamers are strung up on nails in a few walls.

Magenta piñatas hang in a couple trees in the backyard.

Magenta birthday cheers celebrate her son's added year!

Magenta joy commands this wonderful day!

Fuchsia

Fuchsia was his favourite colour.

Fuchsia flowers were planted all around his garden.

Fuchsia shirts filled his closet.

Fuchsia were the walls of his living room, as well.

Fuchsia blossoms were painted over his bedroom wall;
he sometimes dreamed of them.

Fuchsia fields spilled into his mind nearly daily.

Fuchsia, the flower of his dreams.

Fuchsia-coloured cottages.

Fuchsia gardens.

Fuchsia gowns.

Fuchsia fences guard the small structures.

Fuchsia-lovers tend to their homestead.

Fuchsia galas are mere dreams for this family.

Fuchsia dollars are saved for special occasions.

Fuchsia folks hold on to humility until the savored days of mirth.

Fuchsia tea sets collected dust in his China cabinet.

Fuchsia rugs welcomed his guests into his cozy abode.

Fuchsia throw pillows sat on his couch and loveseat.

Fuchsia dinnerware was put on the table for special dinner parties.

Fuchsia flowers sat outside shivering in the cool breeze.

Fuchsia accents appeared in the rest of Adam's rooms.

Fuchsia was adored by him; it is such a nice colour!

Mauve

Mauve lips.

Mauve candy hearts.

Mauve fur coats.

Mauve notebooks in their stationery.

Mauve, fluffy wigs for cosplays.

Mauve walls in their office.

Mauve cupcakes in the kitchen.

Mauve is also the colour of the living room suite.

Mauve is such an odd colour, but is beloved by Tabby, the Fawn.

Mauve is simple to them; it's so feminine but can also be so masculine.

Mauve is so cute!

Mauve flowers.

Mauve skies.

Mauve skin of Lady Ba'vee.

Mauve fabrics and purple stone roads.

Mauve and blue clothes of her little cousin; they swing as she twirls in the street.

Mauve feathers of beautiful pheasants float by as a flock of them fly overhead.

Mauve, shiny shoes with rhinestones crush soft soil underneath them.

Mauve in all shades is Ba'vee and her cousin, Morla.

Mauve is their world, shimmering like soft metal.

Mauve are their hearts, almost glistening is the soft sunlight.

"Mauve cotton sandwiches," she muttered.

""Mauve cotton sandwiches?'" he questioned. "What a strange thing to say!"

"Mauve, cotton, sandwiches!" she chirped, holding up a hand stitched sandwich made of purple cloth.

"'Mauve cotton sandwiches!' I get it now!" he cheered.

'Mauve cotton sandwiches' was an idea of Ophelia's since she was introduced to Dr. Forst; she wanted to make him one… or a few.

Mauve was a favoured colour of hers… as was her doctor's.

Mauve roses were planted by her room's window for her to see every day by him.

Mauve is a sweet colour, sweet like him!

Periwinkle

Periwinkle kittens with little stripes.

Periwinkle sweaters and swirly cappuccinos.

Periwinkle fuzzy socks cover her petite toes.

Periwinkle pajamas and soft blue bed sheets.

Periwinkle cookies cool off on her parents' kitchen counter.

Periwinkle stuffed animals crowd the young girl's room.

Periwinkle hearts float around her head; they are for her beloved family.

Periwinkle is her favourite colour; it brightens every moment of her life.

Periwinkle blossoms rose up from the soil.

Periwinkle-dressed girls picked them all to make bouquets.

Periwinkle roses were added to Tabby's bundle; she wanted only the best for her friends!

Periwinkle tap shoes were purchased for the gala.

Periwinkle performers will have their scene!

Periwinkle dancers—all prepared and anxious—await their cue in the exuberant play!

Periwinkle children run amuck in the fields; they were told not to.

Periwinkle flowers, most precious, are being trampled on by the brats!

Periwinkle tea will not be served to them when they get back!

Periwinkle Park will be closing soon.

Periwinkle plants will need some recuperation tomorrow.

Periwinkle adults just shake their heads and smile, chuckling, "Ah, kids! They'll appreciate these days when they grow old!"

Cerulean

Cerulean seas cover the planet.

Cerulean birds fly over them, migrating from island to island.

Cerulean fish swim within the vast oceans.

Cerulean skies float above the scenery.

Cerulean people trek through the brush and forests in every piece of land.

Cerulean glass towers command the metal cities they've built.

Cerulean flowers decorate significant areas.

Cerulean hallowed grounds honor the cosmos the people dwell in.

Cerulean mornings greet the sister suns of the people's hearth.

Cerulean nights bid their dozy hellos to the gemstone moon.

Cerulean worlds reside in the everlasting void of space, teeming with life.

Cerulean nights.

Cerulean gowns.

Cerulean stones cut with diamonds.

Cerulean skulls of glass.

Cerulean-leafed trees of grandeur.

Cerulean silks draped around her shoulders.

Cerulean-tinted glasses with gold rims.

Cerulean reflecting ponds with koi fish swimming inside.

Cerulean goblets and jeweled shoes.

Cerulean sorcery envelopes her graceless castle.

Cerulean, dark eyes leak cursed gold; her power is too great for any creature to cease.

Cerulean goddess of Death and Misfortune waits for more...

Cerulean blood is spilt; the audacity!

Cerulean innards reveal the coveted jewels; he's been lusting over them for far too long to give them up now!

Cerulean beings pick up their friend's pieces; the greedy bastard has taken what he wanted!

Cerulean tears swell; they form literal streams to — hopefully — wash him away.

"Cerulean beasts! I hope the rest of you are exploited!" Rawka shouts, escaping the magic tides.

Cerulean talons form on the fingers of the victim's loved ones; he's surely dead meat now.

Cerulean waters speed towards the killer's feet; they seek utter destruction.

"Cerulean digestion stones belong where they're made — in our GUTS!" G'sala screamed, swinging his sharpened hands.

Cerulean feet and brown, bloodied boots raced through the grey Caverns of the Crystals.

"Cerulean stones should be used for all your magic, sick creeps!" the crooked salesman spat.

"Cerulean magic will kill you if you mistreat it!" Ran'alda screeched, she loved Tara.

Cerulean figures chased the deranged madman.

Cerulean waves knocked him off his feet... the vengeful people finished him.

Indigo

Indigo nights consumed the skies.

Indigo nocturnal birds flew through the misty air.

Indigo shadows hid behind the mountains and trees.

Indigo flowers in the bushes sat patiently for the sun's return.

Indigo silk banners dressed the temples' halls.

Indigo sconces filled the spaces with light.

Indigo cushions lined the fine tables in the dining room.

Indigo lakes floated nearby, suspended in the air by a magical presence.

Indigo magic spells fly from statues of wizards.

Indigo incantations create this picturesque plateau.

Indigo Buntings flutter from tree to tree as a lonely cat watches through a window.

Indigo bed sheets are stacked on top of the new mattress on the bed.

Indigo-coloured flowers sit in a vase on the small, pink dresser nearby.

Indigo and violet pillows sit comfortably on a plush chair.

Indigo blue jeans paired with a white t-shirt and socks are squished by another cat on the floor.

Indigo notebooks lay on a desk by the bedroom doorway.

Indigo bird calls echo in the hall from Angela's phone.

"Indigo Buntings are my favourite bird!" she tells a visiting friend.

Indigo birds are welcome at her new house anytime!

Indigo skies soared above them.

Indigo seas raged around the old vessel.

Indigo serpents thrashed against the wooden boards.

Indigo banners strewn across the sails waved in the stormy winds.

Indigo water splashed onto the decks of their ship.

Indigo flags are nearly torn off by a leaping creature; 'twas a Deepwater Serpent seeking dinner.

Indigo crew members fought with steel and gunpowder throughout the night.

Indigo clouds split the squall apart; the ill weather ceased.

Indigo serpents rushed back home once their fight was over; last night was not for them.

Ebony

Ebony trees fill the vast space.

Ebony houses are scattered among them.

Ebony-coloured creatures protect the dwellers.

Ebony shadows lurk in the crevasses of the land; they tend to keep to themselves.

Ebony, peaceful nights sparkle with bioluminescent flowers and fungi.

Ebony midnight parties, hosted by the friendly dark beings, are a must in every season.

Ebony defenders with their creepy, strange powers are nothing to be afraid of... they are kind in reality.

Ebony flowers bloom in the morning light.

Ebony roses and irises sing their sunlit songs of brilliant rays and nourished chlorophyll.

Ebony stone paths creep through the lavish, dark garden.

Ebony spiders spin their homes among the plants.

Ebony statues of glorious women shadow the garden; one is a goddess of fertility.

Ebony trees fence the spooky area.

Ebony blossoms are regarded as being exquisitely beautiful in their darkness.

Ebony-coloured bricks stand before her.

Ebony shade encapsulates her body.

Ebony black is the tower before her; it pierces the atmosphere with its spire.

Ebony wood covers the barred windows and doors.

Ebony-coloured grasses and weeds fill the sparse fields beside the machine.

Ebony roses and thorny vines crawl up the gigantic walls.

Ebony thoughts of fearful hesitation swell in Lory's mind.

Ebony-shaded dreams of rescuing her mother is the only thing pushing her forward.

Ivory

Ivory sands reflect the sun's heat.

Ivory-skinned tourists turn red in the ultraviolet light.

Ivory sunlight illuminates the shore's rocky ravines.

Ivory-coloured seagulls snatch up wandering crabs for lunch.

Ivory umbrellas provide shade to those humans who prefer to lounge.

Ivory clouds float within the bright sky.

Ivory seafoam rides the sweeping tides.

Ivory seashells hide abalone and scallops inside them; some humans harvest them for meals.

Ivory pearls are collected from oysters by the people, too.

Ivory bird eggs hatch as the clutch's parents protect them.

Ivory sunshine beckons seagrass to life.

Ivory summers wash in with every year's cycle.

Ivory white in colour was the small trailer.

Ivory was her name; she had such promise.

Ivory white was the product; she was hired to care for it.

Ivory pearls and glistening diamonds were the reward.

Ivory dust was loved by clients; they paid handsomely for it.

Ivory was successful in dispensing it to folks, but... something happened.

Ivory white was the material to sell, but Ivory herself changed her mind.

Ivory soap suds cover her body fluff.

Ivory white is the colour of her bathrobe.

Ivory earrings sit beside Dahra's sink.

Ivory white is her toilet's colour, too.

Ivory gems make up her matching necklace.

Ivory eyeshadows make marks on her eyelids.

Ivory hotels await her visitation; she owns several of the town's best places to sleep!

ABOUT THE AUTHOR

My name is Asa! I am an amateur writer in the southern United States that loves art and creating worlds in my head. I've started to write about them a few years ago, and have been enjoying it ever since.

Currently, you can find me on: Facebook.com – Asa Livingston
https://www.facebook.com/profile.php?id=61552350715850

www.ingramcontent.com/pod-product-compliance
Lightning Source LLC
Chambersburg PA
CBHW071817020426
42331CB00007B/1508